"DISCARD"

STEALTH JET FIGHTER:
THE F-117A

Tracey Reavis

HIGH
interest
books

Children's Press
High Interest Books
A Division of Grolier Publishing
New York / London / Hong Kong / Sydney
Danbury, Connecticut

Book Design: MaryJane Wojciechowski
Contributing Editors: Mark Beyer and Rob Kirkpatrick

Photo Credits: Cover, pp. 13, 14 © Photri-Microstock; p. 5 © Erik
Simonsen/Image Bank; p. 6 © Index Stock Imagery; pp. 8, 18 © George
Hill/Corbis; p. 10 © Bettmann/Corbis; pp. 12, 28, 41a © U.S. Air Force
Photo/Staff Sgt. Andy Dunaway; p. 17 © U.S. Air Force Photo/Tech. Sgt.
Marvin Lynchard; p. 20 © AP Wide World Photos; p. 22 © Associated
Press/Newport News Daily Press/AP Wide World Photos; p. 25 © Jay
Freis/Image Bank; p. 26 © U.S. Air Force Photo/Technical Sgt. Brad Fallin;
p. 30 © Corbis; p. 33 © Reuters/Faleh Kheiber/Archive Photos;
p. 34 © Reuters/Dragan Antonic/Archive Photos; p. 37 © Associated Press
Tanjug/AP Wide World Photos; p. 39 © U.S. Air Force Photo/Judson
Broehmer; p. 41b © U.S. Air Force Photo/Master Sgt. Keith Reed;
p. 41c © U.S. Air Force Photo

Visit Children's Press on the Internet at:
http://publishing.grolier.com

Library of Congress Cataloging-in-Publication Data

Reavis, Tracey.
    Stealth jet fighter : the F-117A / by Tracey Reavis.
        p. cm. – (High-tech military weapons)
    Includes bibliographical references and index.
    Summary: Discusses the history and development of the United
States Air Force's Stealth bomber, its design and special features, and
some of the missions it flew in Operation Desert Storm and in
Kosovo in 1999.
    ISBN 0-516-23341-6 (lib. bdg.) – ISBN 0-516-23541-9 (pbk.)
    1. F-117 (Jet fighter plane)—Juvenile literature. 2. United States.
Air Force—Juvenile literature. [1.F117 (Jet fighter plane)] I. Title. II.
Series.
UG1242.F5 R42 2000
623.7'464—dc21

                                                          00.024387

CONTENTS

INTRODUCTION

Shhh, the United States Air Force has a secret! As part of its air firepower, the government has developed a subsonic jet. It's called the F-117A Nighthawk. This jet uses a form of science called stealth. Stealth planes are designed to sneak past the enemy's radar. Once they are past radar, Nighthawks can easily attack enemy targets.

The Stealth fighter was built in 1979 in a large airplane hangar in California. Then it was moved to Nevada, where pilots could take it for many test-flights. The airplane had some problems and even had a few crashes. But after a lot of hard work, the planes were finally ready for battle.

In 1988, the Pentagon finally showed photos of its secret new plane to the public. The Stealth bomber was first used in the Gulf War in 1991. Its success in this war impressed Air Force experts. As a result, stealth technology is now an important part of U.S. military plans for the future.

The **F-117A Nighthawk** took nearly thirty years to be designed and built.

CHAPTER 1

AIR COMBAT

Airplanes were first used as weapons during World War I (1914–1918). These planes were small and had two sets of wings. They were called biplanes. By World War II (1939–1945), planes were faster and had better weapons. There were fighter planes that had guns for weapons. These planes protected ground bases and patrolled the skies for enemy planes. There were also bombers, which carried heavy bombs that were dropped on ground targets.

Airplanes became weapons during World War I (1914-1918).

Radar uses electronic signals to find airplanes in the sky. Their images appear on a video screen.

In 1947, the U.S. government created a section of the armed forces just for air warfare. The Air Force was developed to manage this specific set of weapons.

Today, one goal of the Air Force is to attack and destroy the enemy's weapons. Many types of aircraft carry bombs and missiles to do this. These explosives are dropped on and shot at enemy ground stations to destroy them. To defend against air attacks, opposing forces use radar (RAdio Detecting And Ranging).

Radar uses electronic signals to tell where planes are in the air. The Air Force believed that airplanes able to attack secretly would help weapons to reach enemy targets. Was there a way planes could get past enemy radar without being noticed?

STEALTH AS A WEAPON

The first time someone saw a stealthlike plane was in 1948. Northrop, an airplane manufacturer in California, had developed an airplane called the YB-49 Flying Wing. One day this plane flew a practice flight over the Pacific Ocean. The Flying Wing suddenly popped onto the radar screen. It had not been spotted until it was almost directly over the Air Force base. The technicians were amazed. The plane's smooth, curved surface

By accident, the YB-49 Flying Wing gave airplane designers the idea for a stealth airplane.

had not reflected radar waves back to the base until the last minute. This event marked the beginning of the age of stealth weaponry. Hereafter, the government began to experiment with different airplane designs. However, it took thirty years before a special project was developed to design an airplane that could be completely invisible to radar.

High-Tech Materials

Besides having a smooth surface, there is another way to make a plane seem invisible. There exists a special radar-absorbing material (RAM). RAM is made of chemicals that absorb incoming radar waves.

If RAM is put on the outside of a plane, it causes incoming enemy radar waves to melt into its surface. The radar waves do not bounce back to the enemy's radar. Therefore the plane does not show up on the radar screen. Then the enemy will not know a plane is flying toward it.

If the enemy could not see bombers flying toward it, the enemy would not be able to shoot at the planes. Bombers could fly right to the enemy and drop bombs or shoot missiles at targets. The Air Force knew it would help their missions to have planes that could sneak up on the enemy. They believed they could make such a plane.

DESIGNING AN AIRPLANE

The first step in building a plane is for an airplane designer to draw the plane on paper. This designer is called an aeronautics engineer. Aeronautics engineers know all about how planes fly. They can design planes that look and fly differently. In 1975, the Defense Department's Advanced Research Projects Agency (DARPA) asked several aeronautic companies to make drawings of planes.

The Lockheed Advanced Development Projects division was given a contract in April 1976. They were to build two test planes that could fly. The two models had the top-secret code name "Have Blue."

Airplane designers use computers
to help them design airplanes.

DARPA told them the company with the best
plan and idea would be hired to make the
aircraft.

Eighty people helped put
together the first Nighthawk.

The Lockheed Martin company from Burbank, California, made the best model plane. This plane had some very special features. It had a diamond shape and it sloped in four directions. This design deflected radar. These features would help the plane to do the exact job the Air Force wanted: sneak past enemy radar and destroy the enemy ground weapons.

CHAPTER 2

LET'S BUILD
AN AIRPLANE

In July 1976, Lockheed was given fourteen months to build two stealth planes. Their names were Have Blue. These planes were the first stealth planes to be built. Such planes are called prototypes.

There were about eighty workers in the Burbank, California, company. They put the plane together in an airplane hangar the size of three football fields. There were four teams working on the airplanes. The engineering team made the drawings. The manufacturing team made all the parts of the plane. The inspection and quality control team checked to see if all of the parts fit together and worked properly. Finally, the flight-testing team made sure that the plane would fly the way Lockheed Martin said it would.

The airplanes were built from front to back, standing straight up like a rocket on a launch pad. The pieces were fitted together like a Lego toy. While building the two aircraft, the workers had to follow strict rules. The stealth planes could not fly faster than the speed of sound (supersonic). Flying at supersonic speeds heated the outside of the aircraft. This heat would make the plane show up on a radar screen.

Also, the Have Blue planes had to make very little engine noise. If the engine was too loud, the enemy could hear the plane coming. If these guidelines were followed, the airplanes would not be seen or heard by the enemy until the plane was only fifteen miles

The Stealth carries bombs in its belly.

away. This may seem like a long way away. You might think fifteen miles gives the enemy time to defend itself. However, within a fifteen mile range the stealth could shoot its missiles and drop its laser-guided bombs. The enemy would be defenseless.

The Lockheed Martin teams worked secretly on the stealth planes. One of the secrets to building the stealth was the tools.

The Stealth flew its test-flights from Nellis
Air Force Base, located in Nevada.

Most aircraft have tools specially built to
work on those planes. Because the stealth
project was top secret, the workers used
wooden tools that were thrown away when
the planes were completed. They did not

want any other countries to get this new stealth technology.

The final Have Blue prototypes had a wingspan of 22 feet and 6 inches. It was 47 feet and 3 inches in overall length and 7 feet and 6.25 inches tall. They were built for a total cost of $37 million.

The Stealth Takes Off

To keep the project secret, the Air Force shipped the Have Blue prototypes to the Nellis Air Force Base (AFB) near Las Vegas, Nevada. Here would begin a series of test-flights at Groom Lake. The Groom Lake test facility was far away from other parts of the base. This was a perfect location for the testing of secret aircraft.

The first test-flight of Have Blue was scheduled for the morning of December 1, 1977. A medical helicopter with two paramedics onboard followed the flight in case of an emergency. Test pilot Bill Park was chosen to make this first flight. He had practiced flying the plane on a computer for more than five weeks.

On the morning of the flight, Park sat in the single-seat plane, ready for takeoff.

In the cockpit, Park gunned the engine. The plane roared. He gently rolled the Have Blue out of the hangar. He eased the throttle forward to make the plane move. The plane entered the runway and gained speed. Park lifted the Have Blue into the sky and into U.S. history books.

This first flight was considered a success. Park was able to fly and land the plane. However, both Have Blue planes eventually crashed during flight-tests. The pilots safely ejected from them, but the planes were broken beyond repair. Yet, these prototypes had already done their job. They helped the Air Force learn what stealth planes could do.

The Have Blue test airplanes crashed, but their pilots both ejected safely from the planes.

The Air Force still wanted to keep the plane a secret. They buried the parts of the damaged planes on the grounds of the Nellis AFB. They didn't want anyone to see what this plane looked like. Not yet.

CHAPTER 3

FINALLY, A STEALTH FIGHTER

The next part of the stealth project was to build five new airplanes. These planes would be used to test the stealth's abilities. The Air Force wanted to see how well the planes could fly. They also wanted to know if their stealth planes really were invisible to enemy radar.

The Air Force built five planes for a reason. After the testing, if something needed to be fixed or adjusted, it could be fixed on all of the planes. Lockheed kept records of all of the parts used to fix one plane. Then they fixed the rest of the fleet.

Flight-tests proved that Nighthawks could fly well.

FSD-1 was the name of the first true stealth fighter. It was completed in May 1981. The plane flew for the first time about one month later. The success of this flight helped the Air Force to decide to build the other four planes. Then the Air Force got each plane ready for tests. Of course, the tests needed pilots to fly the planes.

PILOT TRAINING

Pilots who flew the first F-117As were specially trained. Today, stealth jet fighter pilots receive that same special training. First, they must have more than 1,000 hours of flight time in a jet other than a stealth. That's like flying from New York City to Los Angeles 500 times! Only then can they be considered as a possible stealth jet fighter pilot.

Before climbing into a real stealth jet fighter, the pilots train. The training consists of one month of classroom study and hundreds

Air Force pilots used flight simulators to learn how to fly stealth jet fighters.

of hours of flight simulation time. Here they learn how the stealth fighter flies. All planes have different flying traits. Some planes are slow and hard to steer. Other planes need just a push of the "stick" to make them turn quickly. These traits are what the pilots learn during their training. When it's time for combat, stealth pilots are well prepared.

AIRPLANE SYSTEMS

The F-117A stealth jet fighter is a night-attack plane. It is a single-seat aircraft, meaning there is only one pilot. This fighter uses no radio, no radar, nor any lights when flying over enemy territory. The plane has no electronic devices that can be picked up by enemy radar listening stations.

As a night flyer, the F-117A does not carry guns or air-to-air missiles. This plane was not

designed for high-flying tricks and quick turns. It carries two two-thousand-pound bombs in its belly and flies undetected into enemy territory. Once it drops its bombs, it gets out of the area as quickly as possible. All of the things the plane doesn't have help it to be invisible to the enemy.

The Stealth uses its lights only when landing and refueling at night.

What the plane does have are two General Electric F404 turbofan engines that help it to fly at subsonic speeds. These engines are muffled to eliminate the noise. The plane normally flies below 30,000 feet so that its engines produce no water vapor streaks across the sky.

BUTTERING A PLANE

Before the flight-test of each plane, technicians worked hard putting on the radar-absorbing material. This was a special, putty-like substance. It was used to coat the plane's uneven surfaces. They called this job "buttering." When the planes returned to the hangar for further inspection, the RAM had to be taken off so that the doors and panels could be opened. This procedure was repeated for each flight. It was an important part of the testing. If any uneven part was not covered, the plane would show up on radar. In battle,

In 1980, rumors spread about a black warplane that the Air Force was building in secret. Because of the test-flights, people in Nevada often complained about loud noises heard in the night near the AFB. Newspapers reported that the plane might have been a stealth airplane. Everybody was talking about this new plane. Around this time, a plastic model-airplane maker called Testor started making a 12-inch model stealth airplane. You could buy this model at your local hobby shop!

even one small blip on the radar screen could mean that the plane and the pilot might be seen and shot down.

THE WORLD MEETS THE NIGHTHAWK

On November 10, 1988, the Air Force handed out a single, blurry photograph of the stealth fighter. It was now called the F-117A. Pictures of the F-117A were handed out to news stations around the country. They gave some information about what the plane could and could not do. They also said what the plane would be used for. This was big news! Lots of newspapers put the picture of the stealth bomber on their covers the next day, finally proving to their readers that the plane did exist.

Then in December 1989, the Air Force used the F-117A in a real military situation. The Air Force sent six stealth bombers to the northern border of Panama. The mission was to have stealth planes drop bombs in a surprise attack. The United States later learned that Panamanian leader General Manuel Noriega was not where the F-117As were headed. The plans were changed. The stealth planes did not get to show their real power.

Nearly six months later, the nation got to see the F-117A Nighthawk up close. More than 100,000 curiosity seekers visited the Nellis AFB to witness the first public showing of two F-117As. The crowd's "oohs" and "aahs" showed what an exciting new plane the Nighthawk was.

CHAPTER 4

OPERATION DESERT STORM

In January 1991, Iraq invaded its southern neighbor, Kuwait. Both countries are in the Middle East. Because of the invasion, the United States sent in troops to prepare for war. This time the stealth bomber was the U.S. military's weapon of choice.

The United States moved thirty-seven F-117As to an air base in the Saudi Arabian desert. From this base, the stealth fighter sneaked across the Iraqi border. Then it destroyed the telephone center and the central power station in the city of Baghdad, Iraq. This mission was the start of Operation Desert Storm.

When the Gulf War (1991) began, thirty-seven F-117As flew from the United States to Saudi Arabia.

FIREWORKS IN JANUARY

It was early morning in Iraq, nearly 3:00 A.M. on January 17, 1991. In the air, each of the arriving stealth fighters carried a pair of two-thousand-pound laser-guided bombs called GBU-27s. The planes were well armed, but the pilots were still a little nervous. They were about to meet the enemy army, one that was ready with sixteen-thousand missiles. They could only pray that all of the stealth technology really worked.

The F-117A launched a surprise attack on downtown Baghdad. Several bombs were dropped exactly where they had been planned. Because of stealth technology, the F-117As arrived at their target unseen. They didn't have to worry about the enemy. The pilots were able to focus all of their energy on making an exact hit.

Back in the United States, Americans watched the operation on television. The

The F-117A Nighthawk was used to bomb
Baghdad, Iraq, during the Gulf War.

exploding bombs lit up the skies. The Iraqi
army tried to fire back, but they could not see
the stealth planes. They could only fire
blindly into the sky. They missed the planes.
They knew the Americans were out there, but
they couldn't find them.

It took the Nighthawks only 20 minutes to complete three important bombing raids. In all, they wiped out an Iraqi missile station, the army's main communications center, and the city's central power station.

The era of stealth warfare had begun. The Nighthawk had shown what this new technology could do. A stealth pilot could bomb the enemy before it knew what had hit it. It seemed like nothing could beat a stealth bomber.

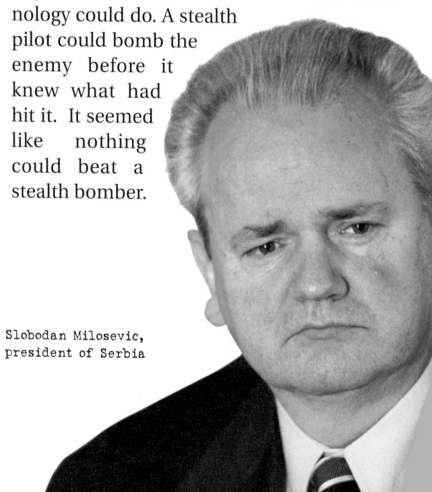

Slobodan Milosevic, president of Serbia

CHAPTER 5

YOUR WINGS ARE SHOWING

The second time the Air Force used many F-117A war planes in combat was in the winter of 1999. The United States fought in Kosovo with a seventy-eight-day air war against the Serbians. Kosovo is a region in the country of Yugoslavia. For many years, violence had been spreading in this region. This violence existed between two groups of people. On one side were the Serbs. On the other side were the Albanians. The Serbs were led by their president, Slobodan Milosevic. The United States peacefully tried to stop

President Milosevic and the Serbian army from harming the Albanians. The Serbs didn't want peace. The United States then began a mission called Operation Allied Force.

In this war, a stealth fighter was shot down for the first time. Television cameras showed Serbian women dancing on the wing of a stealth fighter after it had been shot from the sky. Their government had shot down a U.S. plane! This was a scary sight for Americans. Weren't stealth bombers invisible to radar?

What actually happened is classified information. We can only piece together what is generally known. On the night of March 27, 1999, an F-117A dropped several bombs on a target near Belgrade, Yugoslavia. With its weapons door wide open, the Nighthawk suddenly showed up on the Serbian radar screen. The pilot tried to dodge the enemy attack, but his plane was hit. He stayed with his plane as long as he could. Then he ejected.

On March 27, 1999, a stealth bomber was shot down over Belgrade.

He was later found by American search-and-rescue teams.

In every attack, the stealth bomber has a "buddy plane" in the air with it. While the lead plane is bombing, this second plane jams the enemy's radar. To jam the radar, the buddy plane sends out electronic signals to scramble the radar waves. We do not know if a buddy plane was with the stealth bomber that got shot down. What is known is that stealth

Capt Ken "Wiz" Dwelle

planes are not totally invisible to radar, especially when they open their bomb doors.

STAR WARS IN 2000

Planes used in combat, such as the stealth fighter, make today's video games and science-fiction movie battles seem real. Each war has new technology. For example, almost all of the machinery used in Kosovo during Operation Allied Force included weapons that carried their own laser targeting systems. These systems use laser beams to help aim weapons at targets. In the Gulf War, hardly any weapons had their own laser targeting systems.

The Air Force is always thinking toward the future. It has plans for what to do with weapons that grow old or break down. In fact, the fleet of F-117A Nighthawks is on schedule to be retired from service in the year 2018. Afterward, they will wind up in museums so people can learn about the Nighthawks' history.

The **F-22 Raptor** may replace the **F-117 Nighthawk** as the U.S. military's stealth fighter.

In the meantime, the government has gone back to the drawing board and is designing better weapons. These weapons are kept secret. Rest assured, they are more powerful and better able to hit their targets than those used today. Engineers have created more advanced forms of stealth technology. One plane is being made right now. It is called the F–22 Raptor. This new plane may be completed early in the twenty-first century. Information on this new plane will come out soon. For now, though, the F–22 Raptor is top secret.

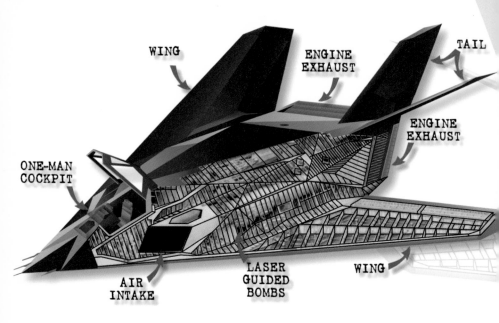

WING

ENGINE
EXHAUST

TAIL

ENGINE
EXHAUST

ONE-MAN
COCKPIT

AIR
INTAKE

LASER
GUIDED
BOMBS

WING

GENERAL CHARACTERISTICS

PRIMARY FUNCTION: FIGHTER/ATTACK

CONTRACTOR: LOCKHEED AERONAUTICAL SYSTEMS CO.

ENGINES: TWO GENERAL ELECTRIC F404

LENGTH: 65 FEET, 11 INCHES

HEIGHT: 12 FEET, 5 INCHES

WEIGHT: 52,500 POUNDS

WINGSPAN: 43 FEET, 4 INCHES

COST: $45 MILLION

CREW: ONE

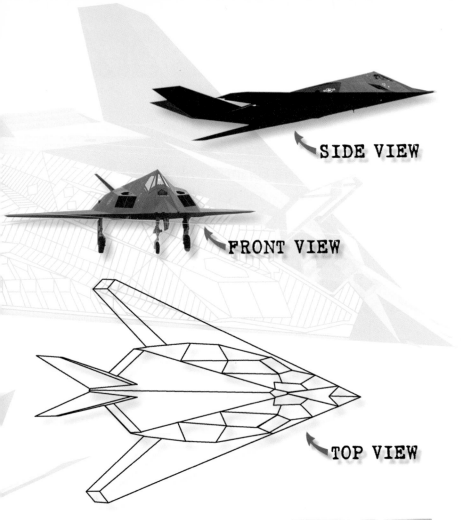

SIDE VIEW

FRONT VIEW

TOP VIEW

PILOT INSIDE COCKPIT

aeronautics a science that deals with flying aircraft

classified not told to the public

communications a system through which information is sent, such as a telephone

curiosity a desire to know

debut a first appearance

deflect to send in another direction

eject to throw yourself out of a plane before it crashes

explosives bombs or missiles used to blow up enemy targets

fatally in a way that causes death

fleet a group operating under one command

hangar a building in which airplanes are kept and fixed

inspection checking or testing a product

paramedic a specially trained medical technician able to provide a wide range of emergency services

Pentagon the headquarters of the U.S. Department of Defense

procedure the steps in which things are done

NEW WORDS

prototype the first working model of a new machine

radar(Radio Detecting And Ranging) a device that sends radio waves that reflect off objects back onto a display screen; used to see objects that are far away

simulation a practice or test that copies what is likely to happen in a real event

stealth the act of being secret; meant to be hidden

subsonic less than the speed of sound in air (761 miles per hour)

supersonic at or above the speed of sound in air (761 miles per hour)

technician a person who has special skills

technology tools or machines used to make or do something

throttle the tool used to control the amount of fuel sent to an engine

veteran a person with a lot of training and experience

wingspan the distance between the wing tips of an airplane

FOR FURTHER READING

Lake, Jon. *Jane's How to Fly and Fight in the F-117A Stealth Fighter (at the Controls)*. San Francisco: HarperCollins, 1997

Holder, Bill and Mike Wallace. *Lockheed F-117 Nighthawk: An Illustrated History of the Stealth Fighter*. Pennsylvania: Schiffer Publishing, Limited, 1996.

Giangreco, D. M. *Stealth Fighter Pilot*. Wisconsin: MBI Publishing Company, 1993.

The Smithsonian National Air & Space Museum
7th & Independence Avenue, SW
Washington, D.C. 20560
202-357-2700
Web site: *http://www.nasm.si.edu*

Web Sites
AV web
www.avweb.com/
This site has tons of top aviation news stories. It includes an auction and shopping area. Membership is free.

U.S. Air Force Museum
www.wpafb.af.mil/museum/
This site has special galleries on early aviation years, weapons, uniforms and trivia. The gallery contains many pictures of different aircraft.

Fighter Planes

www.iaehv.nl/users/wbergmns/jets.htm

Here you can find more than seventy different military aircraft and learn the technical details of each. Contains many pictures and a "most asked questions" list.

INDEX

INDEX

About the Author

Tracey Reavis is a staff writer for the National Basketball Association. She writes for NBA.com, WNBA.com, NBA newsletters and HOOP Magazine.